پرسکون نیند سو جاؤ، ننھے بھیڑئیے

Sov gott, lilla vargen

AF834685

Ulrich Renz · Barbara Brinkmann

پرسکون نیند سو جاؤ، ننھے بھیڑئیے

Sov gott, lilla vargen

ترجمہ:

Muhammad Yahya, Dr. Laila Mushfa (اردو)

Katrin Bienzle Arruda (سویڈش)

sefa

آڈیو بوک اور ویڈیو:

www.sefa-bilingual.com/bonus

مفت رسائی کے لیے پاس ورڈ:

اردو: **Sorry, audio or video is not yet available in this language.**

سویڈش: **LWSV2831**

We are currently working on making as many of our bilingual books as possible available to you as audio books and videos. We kindly ask for your patience if there is no audio or video version in your language yet! You can keep up with the progress of our work on our website:
www.sefa-bilingual.com/languages

شب بخیر، ٹم! ہم کل اپنی تلاش جاری رکھیں گے۔
اب سکون سے سو جائو۔

God natt, Tim! Vi fortsätter att leta imorgon.
Sov nu så gott!

باہر پہلے ہی اندھیرا ہو گیا ہے۔

Det är redan mörkt ute.

ٹم کیا کر رہا ہے؟

Vad gör Tim där?

وہ کھیل کے میدان میں جانے کے لیئے نکل رہا ہے۔
وہ یہاں کیا تلاش کر رہا ہے؟

Han går ut till lekplatsen.

Vad är det han letar efter?

ننھے بھیڑئیے!
وہ اس کے بغیر نہیں سو سکتا۔

Den lilla vargen!

Han kan inte sova utan den.

یہ کون آ رہا ہے؟

Vem är det nu som kommer?

میری! وہ اپنی گیند تلاش کر رہی ہے۔

Marie! Hon letar efter sin boll.

اور ٹوبی کیا ڈھونڈ رہا ہے؟

Och vad letar Tobi efter?

اپنا کھدائی کرنے والا آلہ۔

Sin grävmaskin.

اور نالا کیا ڈھونڈ رہی ہے؟

Och vad letar Nala efter?

اپنی گڑیا۔

Sin docka.

کیا بچوں کو بستر پہ نہیں جانا ہے؟
بلی بہت زیادہ حیران ہوئی۔

Måste inte barnen gå och lägga sig?

Undrar katten.

chez Martin
7
vitrerie

اب کون آ رہا ہے؟

Vem kommer nu?

ٹم کے امی اور ابو!
وہ اپنے ٹم کے بغیر نہیں سو سکتے۔

Tims mamma och pappa!
Utan deras Tim kan de inte sova.

ان میں سے زیادہ تر لوگ آ رہے ہیں!
میری کے ابو، ٹوبی کے دادا اور نالا کی امی۔

Och nu kommer ännu fler! Maries pappa.
Tobis morfar. Nalas mamma.

اب جلدی بستر پہ جائو!

Nu skyndar vi oss i säng!

شب بخیر، ٹم! کل ہمیں مزید تلاش نہیں کرنا ہوگا۔

God natt, Tim!

Imorgon behöver vi inte leta mer!

پرسکون نیند سو جاؤ، ننھے بھیڑئیے!

Sov gott, lilla vargen!

مصنفين

Ulrich Renz was born in Stuttgart, Germany, in 1960. After studying French literature in Paris he graduated from medical school in Lübeck and worked as head of a scientific publishing company. He is now a writer of non-fiction books as well as children's fiction books.

www.ulrichrenz.de

Barbara Brinkmann was born in Munich in 1969 and grew up in the foothills of the Bavarian Alps. She studied architecture in Munich and is currently a research associate in the Department of Architecture at the Technical University of Munich. She also works as a freelance graphic designer, illustrator, and author.

www.bcbrinkmann.de

Do you like drawing?

Here are the pictures from the story to color in:

www.sefa-bilingual.com/coloring

Enjoy!

جنگلی ہنس

مأخوذة عن قصة لهانز كريستيان اندرسن

► Recommended age: 4-5 and up

ہینس کرسٹن اینڈرسن کی کہانی جنگلی ہنس، دنیا کی مشہور ترین بامقصد پریوں کی کہانیوں میں سے ایک ہے۔ یہ کہانی انسانی ڈرامہ کے ہر موضوع ؛ خوف، بہادری، محبت، دھوکہ، جدائی، اور ملن کا بہت خوبصورتی سے احاطہ کرتی ہے۔

Available in your language?

► Check out with our „Language Wizard“:

www.sefa-bilingual.com/languages

My Most Beautiful Dream

► Reading age: 2-3 and up

Lulu can't fall asleep. All her cuddly toys are dreaming already – the shark, the elephant, the little mouse, the dragon, the kangaroo, and the lion cub. Even the bear has trouble keeping his eyes open...
Hey bear, will you take me along into your dream?
Thus begins a journey for Lulu that leads her through the dreams of her cuddly toys – and finally to her own most beautiful dream.

Available in your language?

► Check out with our „Language Wizard":

www.sefa-bilingual.com/languages

www.sefa-verlag.de

IT: Paul Bödeker, Freiburg, Germany

Font: Noto Sans

ISBN: 9783739919164

www.ingramcontent.com/pod-product-compliance
Lightning Source LLC
LaVergne TN
LVHW070602061026
849580LV00018B/2792